Date: 3/17/16

Turkish Van Cats

Kate Conley

**Checkerboard
Library**

An Imprint of Abdo Publishing
abdopublishing.com

abdopublishing.com

Published by Abdo Publishing, a division of ABDO, PO Box 398166, Minneapolis, MN 55439.
Copyright © 2016 by Abdo Consulting Group, Inc. International copyrights reserved in all
countries. No part of this book may be reproduced in any form without written permission from
the publisher. Checkerboard Library™ is a trademark and logo of Abdo Publishing.

Printed in the United States of America, North Mankato, Minnesota.
042015
092015

THIS BOOK CONTAINS
RECYCLED MATERIALS

Cover Photo: Photo by Helmi Flick
Interior Photos: Alamy pp. 9, 21; Glow Images pp. 13, 15; Photos by Helmi Flick pp. 5, 7, 11, 17;
    Jane Burton/npl/Minden Pictures pp. 1, 19

Series Coordinator: Tamara L. Britton
Editors: Megan M. Gunderson, Bridget O'Brien
Art Direction: Neil Klinepier

Library of Congress Cataloging-in-Publication Data

Conley, Kate A., 1977- author.
  Turkish Van cats / Kate Conley.
     pages cm. -- (Cats. Set 9)
  Includes index.
  ISBN 978-1-62403-815-0
1. Turkish Van cat--Juvenile literature. 2. Longhair cats--Juvenile literature. 3. Cat breeds-
-Juvenile literature. I. Title.
  SF449.T88C66 2016
  636.8'3--dc23
                                   2015005166

Contents

Lions, Tigers, and Cats

Cats are members of a large family called **Felidae**. Some are wildcats. These include lions, tigers, cheetahs, and pumas. Others have been **domesticated**. These are the cats that live in homes with people.

Wildcats are different from house cats, but they share many **traits**. They both have large, developed brains and sharp teeth. Cats are strong and graceful when they walk, jump, and run. And, they are meat eaters that hunt their prey.

About 3,500 years ago, ancient Egyptians admired cats and their hunting abilities. They tamed cats to keep **rodents** away from stored grain. Today, cats are popular pets throughout the world. One popular **breed** is the playful Turkish Van.

The Turkish Van cat

Turkish Van Cats

Turkish Vans are an ancient **breed**. They come from the Lake Van area of Turkey. They are also found in parts of Armenia, Syria, Iran, and Iraq. Turkish Vans are one of the earliest-known **domestic** breeds. They have survived unchanged for thousands of years.

These cats remained in their native land for many years. In 1955, two English women started working for Turkey's government. When they returned to England, they brought two Turkish Vans with them. The women began importing more of the cats and breeding them.

Turkish Vans soon became popular in Europe and the United States. The **Cat Fanciers' Association** recognized them as a breed in 1994. Today, Turkey considers these cats a national treasure. So, Turkish Vans can no longer be exported from Turkey.

There are many myths about Turkish Vans. One says that they were mousers on Noah's ark. When the ark reached Mount Ararat in Turkey, the cats jumped out and swam to shore.

Qualities

Unlike most cat **breeds**, the Turkish Van enjoys water. Some Turkish Vans can turn on faucets with their paws. They like to play with running water. Sometimes, they even jump into the shower or bathtub with their owners!

Turkish Vans are often compared to dogs. They can fetch toys, growl, and learn tricks. Turkish Vans can also be taught to walk on a leash.

Despite their similarities to dogs, Turkish Vans like their space. These cats do not like to be handled. They dislike being picked up or cuddled. Turkish Vans make good pets for families with older children and adults.

Turkish Vans are known as "the Swimming Cats" because of their love of water.

Coat and Color

Turkish Vans have white coats. They have red or brown markings on their heads and tails. This type of marking is called the Van Pattern. Some Turkish Vans are solid white. These cats are known as Turkish Vankedisi cats.

The Turkish Van is a semi-long-haired cat. It does not have an **undercoat** like most cats. This makes the coat especially soft. It feels like **cashmere**! The coat is also waterproof.

A Turkish Van's coat changes with the seasons. In the summer, it has a short coat. This keeps the cat cool on hot days. In the winter, it has a long coat. This keeps the cat warm in cold weather.

A Turkish Van may have a mark on the back of its neck. In ancient times, people believed this mark was the "thumbprint of God."

Size

A Turkish Van's soft, white fur covers a large, muscular body. It takes a Turkish Van between three and five years to reach its full size. Adult males weigh 9 to 20 pounds (4 to 9 kg). Females are lighter. They can weigh 7 to 12 pounds (3 to 5 kg).

A Turkish Van has a broad head with a round **muzzle** and a medium-sized nose. Its ears are large with rounded tips. This cat's round eyes are either blue or gold.

Turkish Vans are athletic. They have broad chests, wide shoulders, and long tails. Their legs are strong and set far apart. These **traits** make them great climbers and jumpers. They also help Turkish Vans swim well.

Turkish Vans can have blue or gold eyes. Some are
odd-eyed and have one eye of each color!

Care

Like all cats, your active Turkish Van needs regular checkups. The veterinarian will examine your cat to make sure it is healthy. He or she can also give the cat **vaccines**. And, the vet can **spay** or **neuter** your pet.

At home, a cat needs a **litter box**. The box should be cleaned every day. If this job is not done, the cat may leave its waste elsewhere in the house.

Turkish Vans are always in motion. They have a high level of energy. Turkish Vans love playing with cat toys, especially those that move. This allows them to practice hunting. It also gives them lots of exercise and prevents **obesity**.

Turkish Vans are curious. They need a home that allows them to run, climb, and play with water safely. Items that can break easily should be put away. Toilet lids should be closed so that your cat does not play in the water.

Turkish Vans need little grooming because of their special coat texture.

Feeding

High-energy Turkish Vans often have large appetites. Their food should be healthy. Cats are carnivores. They prefer foods with meat in them. The vet can help a pet owner choose a quality food and a feeding schedule.

Dry cat food is called kibble. It is hard and crunchy. It is common for cats to refuse to eat kibble. Many cats are picky eaters. They prefer moist or wet foods. This is closer to what they would have eaten in the wild.

Moist food comes in a can or a foil bag. Instead of being crunchy, it is soft and chewy. Wet food is similar. It has chunks of meat with sauce over them. Some cats will only eat wet food.

Along with healthy food, cats need fresh water every day.

Kittens

A cat can begin to mate when it is between 7 and 12 months old. After cats mate, the female will be **pregnant** for about 65 days. Then, she will have kittens. The kittens are called a **litter**.

Most cats have litters of about four kittens. The kittens need lots of care from their mother. They cannot see or hear until they are about ten days old. During this time, the mother protects them.

At first, kittens drink only their mother's milk. As they grow older, kittens begin to eat solid food. By the time they are three to four months old, most kittens are able to leave their mothers. They can then be adopted by a family.

Turkish Vans are born with thin coats. Their coats thicken as the kittens grow over the next three to five years.

Buying a Kitten

People buy kittens from many different places. Some kittens come from **breeders**. Others come from families whose older cats had kittens. Still others come from animal shelters. No matter where a kitten comes from, it should be healthy and active.

When a kitten joins a family, it needs some items right away. It needs a **litter box**, as well as food and water dishes. A kitten also needs food. Stores sell food made especially for kittens. This food has the right amount of **protein** to help a kitten grow strong.

As kittens grow, they need places to scratch. A scratching post will stop them from scratching furniture and curtains. Kittens also love to play, so they need cat toys. Plants, jewelry, and other items that are unsafe for kittens to play with should be put away.

It may take some time for your kitten to get used to its new home. With regular care, plenty of love, and good food, your Turkish Van will be an active addition to your family for 15 to 20 years.

A kitten needs a special place to sleep. It should have a soft cat bed. Add a clean towel or blanket for warmth.

Glossary

breed - a group of animals sharing the same ancestors and appearance. A breeder is a person who raises animals. Raising animals is often called breeding them.

cashmere - fine, soft wool from the undercoat of a Kashmir goat of the Himalayan regions.

Cat Fanciers' Association - a group that sets the standards for judging all breeds of cats.

domestic - tame, especially relating to animals.

Felidae (FEHL-uh-dee) - the scientific Latin name for the cat family. Members of this family are called felids. They include lions, tigers, leopards, jaguars, cougars, wildcats, lynx, cheetahs, and domestic cats.

litter - all of the kittens born at one time to a mother cat.

litter box - a box filled with cat litter, which is similar to sand. Cats use litter boxes to bury their waste.

muzzle - an animal's nose and jaws.

neuter (NOO-tuhr) - to remove a male animal's reproductive glands.

obesity - the condition of having too much body fat.

pregnant - having one or more babies growing within the body.

protein - a substance which provides energy to the body and
serves as a major class of foods for animals. Foods high in
protein include cheese, eggs, fish, meat, and milk.

rodent - any of several related animals that have large front teeth
for gnawing. Common rodents include mice, squirrels, and
beavers.

spay - to remove a female animal's reproductive organs.

trait - a quality or feature of something.

undercoat - short hair or fur partly covered by longer protective fur.

vaccine (vak-SEEN) - a shot given to prevent illness or disease.

Websites

To learn more about Cats,
visit **booklinks.abdopublishing.com**. These links are routinely monitored
and updated to provide the most current information available.

Index